BROKEN PROMISES

OF THE

CONSERVATIVES

"Doing the same thing over and over again expecting a different result is insanity" Albert Einstein

BROKEN PROMISES
OF THE
CONSERVATIVES

GENE P. ABEL

authorHOUSE®

AuthorHouse™
1663 Liberty Drive
Bloomington, IN 47403
www.authorhouse.com
Phone: 1-800-839-8640

Published by AuthorHouse   11/17/2015

ISBN: 978-1-4969-1446-0 (sc)
ISBN: 978-1-4969-1444-6 (e)

Print information available on the last page.

Any people depicted in stock imagery provided by Thinkstock are models, and such images are being used for illustrative purposes only. Certain stock imagery © Thinkstock.

This book is printed on acid-free paper.

"Doing the same thing over and over again expecting a different result is insanity" Albert Einstein

Table of Contents

Acknowledgment ix

Preface xi

Foreword xiii

Chapter 1   What is Conservatism? 1

Chapter 2   The nature of conservatism 19

Chapter 3   Broken Promises—Supply Side Economics and Big
             Government is bad...25

Chapter 4   Broken Promises—Social Issues..................51

Chapter 5   Broken Promises—Foreign policy and military issues 57

Chapter 6   Why must the American voter abandon the
             conservatives?..62

About the Author 73

Sources..77

Index...79

Acknowledgment

My sincere thanks to my wife Susan Anne and my friend A. Elliott Rittenhouse for the work they did proof reading and editing my book.

I also want to express my appreciation to the Rev. Nelson H. Rabell—Gonzales, M., DIV., and STM for writing the Forward for my book.

Preface

The conservative movement has become very active in every phase of politics in the United States. The purpose of this book will be to examine what are the conservative principles. How did these conservative movements develop? Document the impact of the conservative policies on the United States.

There are many components that makeup the conservative agenda. In general they can be broken down into three areas. First is the role of government which impacts spending and taxes. A second area is social issues such as abortion, birth control and gay marriage. Finally are foreign policy issues.

The intent of this book will be to enable the reader to understand that repeating the conservative promises and expecting a different result is INSANITY just as Albert Einstein said.

Foreword

Peace. Ret. Colonel Gene Abel's passion and love for justice and equality in our nation is grounded in his ideals of democracy and fairness. As his pastor, when Congress cut billions of dollars from SNAP (Supplemental Nutrition Assistant Program) I heard his concerns for the poor and the economically disadvantage during the prayers of our Sunday service. But Gene is not just a man of words. He has been actively helping people in our community through our congregation's food distribution program that helps more 800 people a month. When he lifted up the cutting of funds from SNAP, he knew how that Congressional action was going to affect the lives of millions of Americans who depend on it. Food pantries throughout the United States, like the one my congregation operates; depend heavily on local State Food Pantries that receive federal funds for their operation. Gene has seen the people who depend from programs like SNAP as a volunteer and donor of our Food Pantry. Sadly, the conservative wing of our political system has not come with a responsible and sensible response to the challenges of countless Americans. Moreover, as Gene points out on this book, the conservative agenda will not only affect the poor but the Middle Class as well. Gene's critical point on this truth-telling book is that we cannot afford a conservative agenda and many will suffer its consequences; from the economically disadvantage through the working class all the way up to the Middle Class. This agenda is flawed and only privileges the wealthiest Americans.

Gene cuts through the false promises and lies of a flawed agenda and provides us with the information and historical perspective needed to stand against it. As a religious leader, I cannot stand silent as I see the future and promise of our children being jeopardized by an agenda that will not provide for most of us, especially the weakest in our society, a chance for a fair chance at a productive and successful life. That's why I agree whole heartedly with Gene. The conservative agenda and its alignment with groups who are anti-gay, anti-immigrant, anti-poor, anti-worker, and pro-rich are at their core anti-human. Thus, as a servant of God, I cannot align myself or give my support to an agenda that will leave division, hatred, and inequality on its wake. Gene has shed much needed light over the true impact of the conservative agenda in our nation and the world. We need to stand up and rise up together, not with hateful hearts, but with hearts full of promise and hope, so that we can lift truth, justice, equality, and peace as the new agenda for our nation. These principles will not fail us, for they promise an abundant life for all. Unlike the Broken Promises of a failed political vision from the extreme right, we need to go back to the principles and ideals of democracy, equality, and compassion. Read this book and lift up your voice. Thanks Gene.

Rev. Nelson H. Rabell-Gonzalez, Senior Pastor at Apostles' Lutheran Church in Turnersville, New Jersey

May 12, 2014

Chapter 1

What is Conservatism?

In a nutshell, conservatism is this idea that government should be minimal with the maximum flexibility for the individual and business to operate without interference. This concept limits regulation, control, oversight and taxation.

Some of these concepts embodied in the conservative agenda can be seen in the golden age of the 19th century when a hand full of wealthy financiers and businessmen all but controlled the economy of the United States. An almost total lack of regulation and control enabled a handful of men such as Cornelius Vanderbilt, Andrew Carnegie, Jay Gould, Pierpont Morgan, and John D. Rockefeller to virtually control the United States. It was at that point that the term "Robber Barons' or the "Captains of Industry" came into vogue. It became clear to President Teddy Roosevelt that the consequences of allowing this small group of powerful and wealthy individuals to do as they pleased would have an adverse impact on the country at large and control the lives of the vast majority of Americans.

http://en.wikipedia.org/wiki/File:Jdr-king.JPG

"Opulence in the Guilded Age, 1890", EyeWitness to
History, www.eyewitnesstohistory.com (2008).

http://www.eyewitnesstohistory.com/gildedage.htm

What the robber barons effectively did was purchase power and
directed untold amounts of wealth into their pockets by funding
friendly politicians to enact legislation that would lower taxes, provide
special tax exemptions, prevent anti-trust regulation and establish tax
loopholes that enabled them to accumulate even more wealth. The
impact of this was to further enhance the wealth of the few at the
expense of the many. Teddy Roosevelt came into a conflict with the very
wealthy Republicans who supported William Taft. Although Roosevelt
was able to limit many of the abuses that were taking place at the turn-
of-the-century Republicans continued to solidify their connections with
large corporations during the presidencies of Coolidge and Hoover. It
would be difficult to identify a conservative Republican who embraces
Terry Roosevelt as a Republican. He was more like a progressive and

was willing to stand up and confront the impending danger rather than simply allow these wealthy individuals to operate as they pleased.

The Political Janus. Offset photomechanical print by Frank A. Nankivell, November 9, 1910. http://hdl.loc.gov/loc.pnp/ppmsca.27682

http://www.loc.gov/pictures/resource/ppmsca.27682/

Although much of the danger that was seen by Teddy Roosevelt with the Captains of Industry was real, it should also be understood that these individuals did produce basic services and industries upon which the economy of the United States was depended for development up until this day. There is no question that these men were ruthless and drove many into bankruptcy by their misuse of power. Labor was treated like slaves during the construction of the transcontinental railroad. In that respect some of the negative impacts of the robber barons were similar to the Robber Barons in the 1500's which is where this term originated. However because of the lasting impact on the development of our economy and industrial base, they are not all negative by any means.

In addition, at the end of their lives these so-called robber barons used their enormous wealth to fund some of the largest examples of philanthropy the world has ever seen such as The Carnegie Institute and the Rockefeller Foundation. Asa Packer who was a coal magnet did much to help found Lehigh University. So to be fair to these robber barons yes they were ruthless and they did cause a lot of harm to a lot of people as they moved forward to develop their enormous power and wealth. However what they created was of significant benefit to our country as a whole and to our population both during and after their lives. Their enormous contribution to the development and welfare of our country should not be ignored while understanding the dangers posed by their concentration of wealth and power.

Compare and contrast these robber barons with their counterparts today who are using the same tactics to accumulate huge wealth but are not creating anything like the substantive worth that we saw from Carnegie, Packer, and Rockefeller etc. Today we have these conservative billionaires manipulating markets creating unsound mortgages to feather their nests. We see the Hunt brothers manipulating the silver industry not to build or create anything of value except to them. One of the most egregious misuses of power coupled with political intervention was a Credit Default Swap in the mortgage collapse that came to a head September 2008.

CDS were developed by a bunch of individuals who hired mathematicians to develop schemes simply to create profit for themselves with absolutely no saving grace whatsoever. At the time these credit default swaps came into being and were used to prop up the bad mortgages, not one person in a million understood what they were or their purpose. However the people who develop the CDS and the politicians that protected them understood. As companies like Countrywide were busy creating designer loans that were unsound from the outset other people decided to sell these Ponzi schemes known as credit default swaps (Source-Two Trillion Dollar Hole by Pam Martens 11/13/2008).

The pitch was for a fee the Credit Default Swap would make a bank or the holder of a bad mortgage whole for any mortgages that went into default. These instruments were written very carefully so as to avoid being legally termed insurance so they would not run into the entanglement of any state insurance laws or commissions.

In September 2000 Senator Phil Gramm(R-TX), the Chair of the Senate Banking Committee, was quoted as insisting that any bill brought to the Senate floor would need to be expanded to include prohibitions on SEC regulation of credit default swap market. In December 2000 it is believed that Sen. Gramm added a provision to an omnibus spending bill that prevented Congress from controlling or having oversight into the sale of credit default swaps (Source-Senate Floor Debate, Senator Gramm 9/14/2000). In essence the federal government was used to provide a guard all shield for those selling these worthless Ponzi schemes. They provided no protection from any losses caused from the bad mortgages that companies like countrywide were developing. The result of selling trillions of dollars of these credit default swaps was to put into jeopardy the nature and existence of AIG the world's largest insurance company. AIG was involved with almost every major corporation in the United States. Because of the risk that these credit default swaps posed to AIG as well as to Goldman Sachs the entire economic system of the United States was put into peril. This was the reason that AIG and others received hundreds of billions of dollars of bailout through the TARP program.

Except for the potential failure of the nine largest banks in the fall of 2008, the failure of AIG and Goldman Sachs would've been the next most serious financial issue facing our country. The corruption and misuse of power and the entanglement of government to allow this misuse to occur is one of the most damning of the broken promises of conservatives today.

Up until the economic collapse in the fall of 1929, it appeared as if the policies we were following which allowed large corporations and the very wealthy to operate in an unbridled fashion and without responsibility was producing prosperity for our country. The truth is that what it was doing was setting the stage for the most fundamental economic catastrophe this country has ever encountered—The Great Depression (Source-Bureau of Labor Statistics Historical Tables). The dimensions of the economic morass created by the Great Depression are hard to imagine since very few people today lived through it. We had a country literally brought to its knees and had somewhere in the range of 25 to 30% unemployment as compared with the April 2014 rate of 6.3% and if you added underemployment in 1929 you would have reached more than 50% at the depths of the Great Depression.

We had people living on the streets standing in line waiting for a piece of bread and a small bowl of watered down soup. People who formally had worked hard and had a reasonable net worth were wiped out in a matter of several days. We had shantytowns constructed in major cities of our country because people had nowhere to live. All of this occurred because we allowed the unbridled misuse of money and power by wealthy individuals and large corporations in the years leading up to the fall of 1929. As bad as the market crash was on 27 October 1929 the bank failure in many cases was even worse. It impacted people that were of even more modest means who had their life savings in the banks that one day closed never to reopen.

My family had personal experience with this phenomenon when the Dime Savings Bank in Allentown Pennsylvania closed never to reopen. My great-grandmother on my maternal side lost, for the most part, all of her liquid assets when the Dime Savings Bank failed in 1933. There were millions of Americans who lost all or most of what they had when the banks failed.

http://en.wikipedia.org/wiki/File:American_union_bank.gif

We had no FDIC and no effective Federal Reserve. We had a system that for the most part allowed banks to take risks and operate without regulation without control and that excess along with the excess in the stock market all but destroyed the economy of the most powerful nation on earth and brought with it a worldwide depression. Many conservatives today change the subject or refuse to knowledge that speculation and lack of effective regulation are the principal reasons why the Great Depression happened in the United States. They ignore the hands off administrations of Coolidge and Hoover enabled the Great Depression to take place.

In January 1933 Franklin Delano Roosevelt was faced with a situation that, left unchecked, could have produced a system that would be more accurately described as a plutocracy. This group of the very wealthy and powerful people got the right politicians in office and judges on the courts to protect their wealth and power. Only the widespread economic consequences which came to light in the fall of 1929 and came to a head with the bank failure in early 1933 caused the people in this country to vote for progressive candidates and recognize the illusion that was created by Coolidge and Hoover and their conservative agenda that resulted in the Great Depression.

The concept of "the best government is the least government" which is one of the principal tenets of a conservatism was actually shown to be ineffective long before the 1900s and the robber barons. During the first 15 years of the United States the government structure that we adopted under the Articles of Confederation where the central government had almost no power or authority proved to be unworkable. It was because of that that realization that the Constitution replaced the ineffective Articles of Confederation in 1789.

Even though the Constitution passed in 1789 significantly strengthened the Federal Government through federalism much of the power was still in the hands of the individual states. Over the years it became clear that as the United States changed from an agrarian society to a manufacturing and commercial society we needed to have more uniform procedures in order to grow and prosper. We could not afford 50 different sets of rules dealing with the growing economy and world commerce. Our Pledge of Allegiance clearly states, "One **nation** under God, indivisible with liberty and justice for all." We are not **50 nations** and the Liberty and Justice for All should be the same no matter which state we choose to live in and raise our families.

The Constitution provides to the states the authority not specifically enumerated in the Constitution to the Federal Government. The growth in power that was needed for the country to prosper and grow and effectively deal on the world stage was achieved under the Commerce Clause in the Constitution. Whenever something related to the commerce of the country at large the Federal Government trumps state law and regulation. If it were not for that interpretation, it is hard to imagine how the United States would function as ONE NATION!

Those that claim we should get back to the founding fathers' employ rhetoric that although it sounds good it is in effect meaningless. Our country today is nothing like the country in 1776 or 1789 and if the founding fathers had been faced with the reality of the 21st century, I doubt very much that the Federalism that we have in our Constitution would exist to the extent that it does today.

So from the very founding of our country, the concept that we can allow individuals, companies and states to go it alone and do as they please has been proven to be not only ineffective but on a number of occasions disastrous. It is hard to know if Teddy Roosevelt had not confronted the robber barons what would've happened at the turn of the century. We know the result of lack of control and the concept that business knows best under Coolidge and Hoover which resulted in the Great Depression. The near depression in 2008 is the most recent example of the same lack of regulation.

HOOVER CARTOONS

Description: Cartoon by Clifford K. Berryman, published in the Washington Evening Star, 1917

Herbert Hoover Presidential Library and Museum

http://www.hoover.archives.gov/info/Food%20Relief/1917-58.html

http://www.ushistory.org/us/36b.asp

None of us today truly understand how serious the financial crisis our country was in between the fall of 1929 and early 1933. Many of the statistics that we have today did not exist in 1929 and it is difficult to really know the true extent of the unemployment and the underemployment that resulted by allowing unbridled speculation and irresponsible profiteering that took place prior to the fall of 1929.

It took the very aggressive centralization of government authority to begin taking our country back to a position of reason. The fact of the matter is we did not fully come out of the Great Depression until the Second World War. Actions like the CCC, WPA, rationing, price controls all were necessary to overturn the consequences that the laissez-faire policies of the Republicans under Coolidge and Hoover produced. The irony is that when the Great Depression took place many of the very wealthy lost much of their power and wealth power. The unfortunate thing is that people who never had the power and the wealth also found they had almost nothing. This country had soup lines and shantytowns which were dubbed Hoovervilles. People who lived in these Hoovervilles begged for food. There structures were made from wood from crates and cardboard or anything else that was available.

HOOVERVILLE

http://en.wikipedia.org/wiki/File:Hoooverville_williamette.jpg

Despite the horrifying consequences of the Great Depression in 1929 we allowed ourselves to again jeopardize the economic system of our country with the policies we began to follow in 2001. We developed a similar scenario to the pre-1929 agenda when it appeared as if the economy was reasonably sound in the early part of the Bush administration up to late 2006 when the storm clouds became evident. The deficit of course began almost immediately and continued to grow with his tax cuts but the impact of the mortgage and investment bank abuses did not become evident until 2007. By September 2008 this country was on the brink of another Great Depression. We were within days of having our banks fail and the shutdown of the economic system of our country. In the days that led up to TARP, which was developed by Sec. of the Treasury Paulson, banks were in a position where they would not lend money to any person for any reason.

In the meetings that were held with George W. Bush and congressional leaders, Bush was told that if action was not taken to prop up the nine largest banks as well as AIG there was almost 100% probability of a financial catastrophe similar to 1933. In fact, it was reported at one of those meetings Sec. Paulson said to Bush that if he failed to act and convince Congress to pass TARP that he could very well have the legacy similar to Herbert Hoover except that the shantytowns that would result would be called Bushvilles.

http://en.wikipedia.org/wiki/File:President_George_W._Bush_bipartisan_economic_meeting_Congress,_McCain,_Obama.jpg

Here again we saw the conservative ideology come into direct conflict with dealing effectively to prevent another Great Depression. When push came to shove 6 Republicans voted with the Democrats to pass TARP and prevent a bank failure and the failure of AIG (Source-Politico 10/3/2008). The conservatives argued that the free market should deal with the problem which was tantamount to saying that they should allow the banks and AIG to fail and the consequences that followed would be better than dealing with the crisis. It is hard to understand how any philosophical belief could be as fundamentally wrong as to risk repeating a situation similar to 1933.

It is important that we all understand just how serious of an economic morass was created by allowing big business and wealthy individuals to operate without reasonable and effective controls. Only in that way can we hope to prevent such a re-occurrence again. If today, the United States fell into an economic situation similar to the Great Depression the global impact would be nothing less than catastrophic for the entire planet.

Chapter 2

The nature of conservatism

Although many of the tenets that comprise the conservative agenda in 2014 have existed in the past, the coalition of groups and individuals pushing these ideas has increased in intensity and ineffectiveness. Huge amounts of money from a few wealthy conservatives and a tactic of doing and saying almost anything in order to foster the conservative ideology has produced some very disturbing consequences.

Conservatism can be grouped into three specific areas. First, are the social conservatives which coalesce around things such as birth control, abortion and gay marriage and issues that relate to religious conviction rather than economic or foreign policy. Another group of conservative ideas centers around the role of the United States plays on the world stage with regard to foreign policy and military intervention. For the most part the Neocons, as they are known, are pushing a military solution to resolve many of the difficulties that exist throughout the world. The final and probably the most fundamental issues revolve around the role of government which in turn dictates spending and taxes.

In general, the issues that are dubbed of a social nature and that are based on religious belief are less subject to some of the broken promises that we see in the other two categories, foreign policy and the economy. Conservatives however are trying to enforce their ideology on everyone. It is not satisfactory to simply hold these beliefs and practice them as they choose but rather to impose their beliefs on everyone else. A good example is the attempt to try and limit help to Planned Parenthood because of the belief that Planned Parenthood helps women with birth control and abortion should the women choose that option.

Certainly the convection surrounding abortion and when life begins is a very fundamental issue and one that is difficult to deal with in the 21st century. Medical science and technology has enabled us to do things that heretofore were not possible or practical. Therefore it is easier for women to opt for abortion to deal with an unwanted pregnancy or to utilize various methods of birth control to prevent the pregnancy in the first place. There is no argument that conservatives, as well as any other group, is certainly entitled to their individual belief and practice with respect to their sexuality, birth control and who they choose to love and be with. The issue is that the conservative movement attempts to impose their particular belief on everyone.

Free Will is granted to each person by God and should not be decided by anyone even when it deals with birth control or abortion. Some in the conservative movement believe that the sexuality of a person is a learned trait. This is simply incorrect and science has established the fact that homosexuality is a reality both in human species as well as in other species.

This idea was held by Michelle Bachmann and her husband who fostered a clinic to reeducate gays so that they would become heterosexual (normal to conservatives). This is a perfect example of the conservative movement trying to impose what they believe on others. They do so despite the fact that the science simply does not support their particular belief and despite the reality that God gave each of us are own free will.

This is true of the global warming issue where 98% of the world scientists believe that the earth is warming and the vast majority of that 98% also believe that the actions of man burning hydrocarbons and increasing the CO2 levels is accelerating the climate change. Despite the fact that 98% of the worlds scientists are in agreement and that we have indisputable facts that show that the temperatures of the oceans have risen, that the polar caps are melting and the level of the world's oceans have risen, conservative groups insist this is untrue and belittle science and the empirical data that proves climate change is taking place on planet Earth (Source-Scientific American 1/10/2014). The most likely reason conservatives are ignoring this reality is that to curb the amount of hydrocarbons pumped into the atmosphere more regulation, higher taxes and increasing costs for many businesses would be needed to implement solutions that will reduce carbon emissions.

The downside of ignoring the global warming issue could be nothing less than catastrophic. There are two very important components that must be addressed to avoid this catastrophe. We need defensive measures in low-lying areas to protect those areas from storm surges because the oceans are rising. Areas like New York, New England, the Gulf Coast and Florida are becoming increasingly vulnerable to the damage caused by the disruption of the Earth's weather patterns and the fact that the oceans have risen and will continue to rise. Unless we act like Holland and England within 50 to 100 years we will not be able to use many of our coastal areas. The financial hardship this will cause the United States is unimaginable.

The second issue is how can we slow the onslaught of this climate change to not only give us the time to provide for some defensive measures but also to reduce the magnitude of the defensive measures that may be necessary. We need to protect the two thirds of the population that live along coastal areas. The downside of ignoring global warming will be the most fundamental mistake this country has made in its entire history. To envision the United States without New England, New York, the Gulf Coast, Florida and parts of California is unfathomable. We simply cannot risk allowing the conservative tactics to ignore the consequences of this issue. The consequences are such that we will be unable to continue as a world power and to enable our country to maintain its freedom if we had the catastrophic financial impact of losing our coastal areas because of rising oceans and the damage caused by ever intensifying storms.

We have other groups of conservatives who also argue that the earth and man is about 6,000 years old despite the fact that there is indisputable scientific evidence that life existed on the earth for hundreds and hundreds of millions of years. These conservative groups argue that there is no such thing as evolution and that about 6,000 years ago everything that we see from the simplest plant to the most complex organisms began. We see attempts by the conservatives to impose their ideas on others. The effort in Texas to change the textbooks to remove evolution is another good example of why conservatives insist that what they believe should be believed and accepted by everyone despite the fact that their beliefs are simply unsupportable by scientific data and facts.

Certainly there are no more compelling examples of how conservatives generally either ignore factual data that disproves their ideas or distorts actual data to make it appear as if their positions on various issues are valid. One of the tactics that is used is to repeat unsupportable statements and lies over and over again so that eventually people will begin to believe that there may be some truth in the statements that are being made.

There is no question that this tactic has worked and convinced many otherwise logically thinking individuals that what the conservatives claim is the truth regardless of the evidence in factual data to the contrary. Another tactic that is used is to attempt to change or alter history or to make it appear as if something that has been documented simply didn't happen. Several examples that fall into this category are things like ignoring the impact that speculation and unbridled and irresponsible actions by wealthy individuals and large corporations had on enabling the Great Depression in 1929 (Source www.history.com/topics/1929-stock-market-crash).

Today we have people blaming the fact that the federal government encouraged homeownership and that this caused the millions of failed mortgages that began to take place beginning in early 2007. The fact of the matter is that homeownership for people who are qualified and financially able to own a home is the most powerful stimulus for our economic welfare and growth. What caused the unbelievable debacle in the real estate and mortgage industries are the unsound mortgages that were created from 2002 to 2006. Approximately 90% of the bad mortgages were created during that time period (Source-www.history.com/topics/1929-stock-market-crash). People that should not have been given mortgages because of their financial inability to pay the mortgages were made. The so-called designer mortgages and "no doc" loans enabled buyers to gain approval for mortgages that were far in excess of what they can actually be expected to pay in the long run. This was done by unscrupulous mortgage companies to increase their profits by increasing the size of the mortgage granted to individuals. Some of these mortgages started with a $1,000 a month payment and then jumped to $2,000 a month after three years and then to $3,000 per month after five years. What the mortgage originators did was qualify the person only for the $1,000 payment ignoring the likelihood that they would not be able to increase their mortgage payment over a five year period by 300% (Source-U.S. Department of Statistics).

The "no doc" loans were granted without verifying income, employment or any other basic information prior to granting the mortgage. All the buyer had to do was put a down payment of 20% or more of the purchase price. When real estate prices began to fall many of these "no doc" loans wound up underwater because the 20% equity that they established all but disappeared when the value of their real estate dropped by 40 or 50%.

If every one of the mortgages that have been created in the 2002-2006 had been given to people that were qualified buyers, we would not have seen the huge default of millions of mortgages that took place starting in early 2007 and triggered the largest economic downturns since the Great Depression. The issue was not as conservatives claim that the government encouraged people to buy homes that caused the default on the mortgages. The issue is that mortgage originators, rating companies and mortgage re-purchasers such as Fannie and Freddie Mac allowed millions of unsound mortgages to be created. The lack of effective regulation and oversight allowed the creation of these unsound mortgages.

Chapter 3

Broken Promises—Supply Side Economics and Big Government is bad

Beginning with the 1980 presidential campaign we heard a great deal about the change that conservatives were trying to initiate with respect to the size of government, taxes, welfare reform and a whole host of the issues that conservatives embraced. Very often when we apply a title or name to something as multifaceted as political ideology we can misstate or misapply the term to certain groups or individuals. This is certainly true with the term conservative or for that matter liberal.

The conservative ideology can be grouped into three basic categories. The first category of issues that conservatives support is like the doorway to their Temple. One pillar is the idea that we have very limited government and that the free market is best suited to make the decisions without government interference. The second pillar is this idea of supply-side economics where we tax the wealthy at a very low rate with the promise of trickle-down economic benefit to the remainder of our citizens. The second category is the social issues which include birth control, abortion, women's healthcare, help for the poor, disabled, students and gay-rights. Finally the third area relates to the foreign policy issues and the use of our military to impose solutions in the world's trouble spots. Today Terrorism is the major danger we face while Communism was the issue during the 1960-1980's. There are some people who would consider themselves conservatives who support the conservative position in all of these categories while others concentrate on only some of these policies.

For example, the most extreme group regarding the role of government are the Libertarians which for the most part would have very little government of any sort. Many of the people in this particular category do not have a strong feeling about some of the social issues. Nevertheless, all of these policy areas are in stark contrast to what most progressives embrace and the reasons we are having such political discord. There is very little middle ground given the extreme differences between what the conservatives would have us do and what the progressives want. American politics in 2014 is like having a switch that has two positions on or off. There is no dimmer switch especially with respect to what the conservatives are willing to accept.

One of the most fundamental issues comes from the first category and deals with the concept known as supply side economics. During the 1980 campaign, Ronald Reagan made a very effective argument that in essence says by lowering the tax rates for the upper income Americans we would stimulate economic growth and provide a stronger economy. The idea was that the wealthy would utilize their additional resources from lower taxes to invest in businesses, create jobs and the benefits would trickle down from the top to the middle class and provide a broadening of the economic benefits.

This concept was dubbed "Reaganomics" and it was a very significant departure from what we had been doing and from the theory that most economic growth and prosperity is a factor of demand and spending. Certainly we did not have a lack of capital for business investment prior to 1981 when we had significantly higher tax rates on the upper income tax payer. American Business never lacked the capital it needed to grow and expand.

Ronald Reagan was a very effective speaker and his ability to sell his supply-side economics and the smaller government concept probably stems from his years as an actor in Hollywood. During the debates of the 1980 presidential election he was very effective in convincing both the American voter and later the Democrat controlled Congress to put in place his ideas. This came at a time when we had relatively high taxes which had been even higher in the 40s, 50s and 60s because of the horrendous cost that the Second World War placed on the United States.

http://en.wikipedia.org/wiki/File:Carter_Reagan_Debate_10-28-80.png

President Reagan convinced Congress to enact his plan to reduce the top tax rate from 70% to 28% and end the indexing for inflation that had been part of the tax law. The impact on the revenue from these changes was huge and President Reagan understood that initially there would be an annual budget deficit because of the loss in tax revenue.

The two promises that were made by conservatives were if we cut the tax rates as President Reagan wanted, by 1985 growth in economy would restore the lost revenue due to the tax cuts and the budget would be balanced. The second promise was that the benefits would trickle down to the middle class with job and GDP growth and produce economic benefits for all Americans due to the tax cuts for the wealthy.

As expected, the annual budget deficit began to grow and continued to grow through the entire term of President Reagan's eight years in office. Below per the Bureau of Public Debt, Department of the Treasury are the actual results from the implementation of Reaganomics:

Year	Annual Budget Deficit*
	(Amounts in Billions)
1981	86
1982	134
1983	231
1984	218
1985	266
1986	283
1987	222
1988	253
Total	1,693 ($1.7 Trillion)

*Does not include revenue or expense from Social Security or Medicare. Source OMB Historical

Table 1.4

The total impact on the National Debt during the eight years of Ronald Reagan presidency after passing his huge tax cuts, took the debt from approximately $907Billion to $2.6 Trillion. That is an increase of almost 300% in eight years

Clearly the promise that by 1985 the budget would return to be in balance after the Reagan tax cuts was not kept. The reason that the promise failed is because the growth and the trickle-down to the middle class in the form of better paying jobs and more benefits to middle-class Americans failed to materialize in anything close to what Ronald Reagan had promised when selling his supply-side economics to the American voter and to Congress. **Thus, both the promise of a balance budget and the trickle-down benefits to the middle and lower income Americans simply never happened. What did happen is the wealthy became wealthier and the indebtedness of the country tripled (Source-www. treasurydirect.gov/govt/reports/pd/histdebt/histdebt.htm).**

If the impact of failing to keep these two conservative promises from the Reagan tax cuts had ended when Ronald Reagan left office, their impact would not have been so devastating on the United States. The truth of the matter is that Ronald Reagan was very disappointed by the budget deficits and agreed to raise taxes several times in the latter part of his administration in order to reduce the ever-growing deficit that resulted from his 1981 tax cuts.

The irony is that any Republican candidate that acted like Ronald Reagan who admitted his mistake and increases taxes to help move the budget back toward balance would be crucified by the conservatives. Can you imagine any of the leading conservative Republican candidates in 2016 that would support increasing taxes in order to help balance the budget? Any such assertion by a Republican candidate today would be the kiss of death. Although most Republicans have canonized Ronald Reagan anyone acting like Ronald Reagan in the latter part of his presidency could not be elected Republican dogcatcher today.

When George H. W. Bush was elected president and took office he made his famous promise, "read my lips no new taxes". President Bush quickly learned that even with the increase in taxes that Ronald Reagan approved it was not possible to bring the budget to balance given the tax rates that were in place when he took office. Bush 41 was probably the last major Republican leader who was truly a fiscal conservative. When he saw it was not possible to move toward a balanced budget given the low tax rates, he went back on his promise and raised taxes in order to help move the country toward a balanced budget. For him, balancing the budget was the prime directive as it would be for any truly fiscal conservative person. **The so called fiscal conservatives today are nothing of the sort. They are simply anti-tax.**

In addition to the added revenue from the Bush tax increases, we saw President Bush reduce spending especially on the military taking advantage of the peace dividend after the collapse of the Soviet Union. The rate of increase in the national debt began to slow and by the end of Bush 41's term in office the national debt stood at approximately $4.1 Trillion. Thus in his four years the national debt rose approximately $1.1 Trillion. **Nevertheless when George Herbert Walker Bush left office the United States was still running an annual budget deficit of about $380 billion per year (Source-www.treasurydirect.gov/ govt/reports/pd/histdebt/histdebt.htm).**

When President Bill Clinton took office, he also found that even with the increases in taxes from Ronald Reagan and Bush 41, we were still running substantial deficits. Even the spending cuts were not sufficient to return the budget to balance. As a result Bill Clinton, like his two predecessors, increased taxes and further cut spending especially on the military in order to bring the budget into balance. The annual budget deficit continued to drop and by 2000 we had the first balanced budget in decades. **It took 18 years to end the annual deficits the Reagan tax cuts created.**

The cumulative impact of the Reagan tax cuts on the national debt was to take our national debt from $900 billion in 1980 to $5.7 trillion in 2000. Thus, the real impact on the national debt from the disastrous Reaganomics was almost $5 trillion increase in the national debt.

The long-term consequences of increasing the national debt by $5 trillion, assuming that the interest we would have to pay is about 5% would be $250 billion a year in added interest. Although today we have very low interest rates according to the Department of the Treasury Bureau Public Debt, the average that we have paid on our public debt over the years averages about 5%. There is no reason to believe that in the long run we will not see the cost to finance our national debt return to that 5% rate. So the actual impact of just the Reagan experiment with supply-side economics has had a huge impact on our budget and will continue to do so until we have repaid that debt. If interest rates were to go above 5%, as they were during the early Reagan years, the negative impact on our budget will be even greater.

In 2001 George W. Bush became our first president with an MBA from Harvard, none the less. In 2001 President Bush argued that we had a projected surplus in the neighborhood of $6 trillion that would materialize between 2001 and 2011. He therefore reasoned that we were overtaxing the American taxpayer because of this $6 trillion projected surplus and proposed his 2001 tax cuts to Congress. **The Bush tax cuts were to stimulate the economy, create jobs and trickle down to the masses. It was precisely the same promises that Ronald Reagan made 20 years earlier.**

The 2001 Bush tax cut was designed to benefit the top 10% of taxpayers. **We were given a warning from none other than Alan Greenspan, chairman of the Federal Reserve that we should never again return to annual budget deficits now that we had finally balanced the budget. In fact Alan Greenspan, a lifelong Republican, said that if** the proposed tax cuts were passed and we again returned to annual budget deficits that the tax cuts should be rescinded (Source-www. reprints.longform.org/alan-greenspan-hylton 1/25/2001). At the same time the two wealthiest men on earth, Bill Gates and Warren Buffett, sent a letter to President George W. Bush recommending he not cut the tax revenue by lowering income tax rates. They said we had far more important things to do with the money. Bush insisted that we were overtaxing the American public and justified giving most of the tax cuts to the wealthy since the wealthy were the ones that pay most of the income taxes.

President Bush and the Republican controlled House and Senate passed the 2001 tax cut which lowered taxes primarily on the wealthiest Americans. **The result of the 2001 Bush tax cuts was to immediately cause the annual budget deficit to return.** We went from a small surplus in 2000 to a $100 billion deficit in 2001. In 2002 that deficit jumped to $360 billion. Even with a strong economy, the Bush tax cuts caused a return to annual budget deficits. Rather than follow the advice of Alan Greenspan and rescind the 2001 tax cut, George Bush and the Republican-controlled Congress passed a second tax cut in 2003 and the deficit began growing even faster. Then GWB invaded Afghanistan and Iraq which increased military spending and drove the annual budget even higher. **By the end of the eight years of the Bush presidency the annual budget deficit stood at over $1.5 trillion.** George W. Bush pushed the national debt from the roughly $5.7 trillion when he took office to $11.9 trillion. That is an increase of more than $6 trillion which is the exact amount that Bush claimed in his projected surplus. The truth of the matter is there was no surplus and again we applied of the same conservative supply-side economics that produced the same result. What a surprise!

Thus the conservatives tried their supply-side economics three times by cutting taxes in 1981, 2001 and 2003. Each time the conservative promise of a balanced budget and trickle-down benefits failed. Each time we got the very same result even though the promise of the conservatives was to give us the opposite result. When you look at the magnitude of the increase in the National Debt that doing the same thing over and over again did to our indebtedness the lunacy of the conservative agenda with respect to our budget and our national debt is irrefutable. **This is not opinion. This is not theory. It is what happened when we cut revenue to the point where we could no longer pay for the spending that the Congress and the President agreed to spend each and every year.** This increase in the National Debt had absolutely nothing to do with either Social Security or Medicare. In fact during the period from Ronald Reagan through Bush 43, both Social Security and Medicare generated annual surpluses. **Although these entitlement programs are definitely a long-term funding issue they played absolutely no part in taking our national debt from less than $1 trillion in 1980 to just under $12 trillion in 2008. Most of the increase in our debt is because of the failed conservatives Supply-Side Economics. Add to that the increased spending on two wars conservatives refused to fund with added tax revenue.**

In 2009, Barack Obama was handed the largest budget deficit in our history. In addition, the economy was on the brink of another 1929. He was also confronted with a challenge from the Republicans to the Minnesota Senatorial seat of Al Franken. This prevented Democrats from controlling the 60 votes in the Senate to stop Republican Filibusters. For the first five months of President Obama's term in office, nothing of substance passed in the United States Senate because the Republicans employed the filibuster to prevent a vote. There is no question the policy changes would have been approved by the Senate if it had come to a vote but this parliamentary maneuver known as filibusters that requires 60 votes to bring a bill to a vote continued the policies of George W. Bush.

In addition to the inability to increase taxes or pass a Stimulus package in January 2009, President Obama was faced with the added cost of the two Bush wars which were raging at a cost of hundreds of billions of dollars per year. The near depression President Obama inherited from George W. Bush meant that millions of Americans who lost their jobs were no longer paying income taxes and began drawing welfare benefits because of the unprecedented economic disaster that George W. Bush handed his successor.

In May 2009, the disputed Minnesota seat was settled and Al Franken was seated as the 60th Democratic Senator. At that point President Obama began by passing his economic stimulus measures to reverse the economic downturn he had inherited. The Democrat controlled House and Senate passed a stimulus package which was approximately $800 billion. It was equally split between tax cuts to the middle class, direct payments to the states and infrastructure repair projects. By the time the stimulus package began to show some impact we were at the beginning of the second year of President Obama's first term in office. Conservatives claimed that the stimulus package would not work and was not needed. The fact remains, by the second year of President Obama's term we saw an end to the loss in jobs and a reduction in the annual budget deficit from the $1.5 trillion level that he inherited in 2009 to $ 650 Billion in 2014. The Stimulus did work even though most economists believe, given the magnitude of the recession Bush handed Obama, the stimulus was too small (Source-The Economist 10/4/2012).

In November 2009 the special election to replace the late Ted Kennedy's seat in the Senate produced a shock to President Obama when a Republican, Scott Brown, was elected to fill the balance of Ted Kennedy's term. At that point the remainder of any changes to help stimulate the economy or reform our tax laws came to an end because Republicans again return to their tactic of filibustering almost everything President Obama proposed. The consequence was President Obama became almost like a Lame Duck one year into his first term. The national debt continued to grow at a slower pace. By 2014 the national debt stands at $17 ½ trillion dollars. The inability to further stimulate the economy and increase tax revenue by restoring tax rates to a more reasonable level and ending tax loopholes has extended the tax policies enacted by Bush and the conservatives. This has prevented us from balancing the budget and continued increasing the National Debt from $12 Trillion in 2009 to $17.5 Trillion today.

The bottom line of the conservative promise that supply-side economics and cutting taxes on the wealthiest taxpayers would balance the budget and grow the economy to the benefit of the middle class has been an abject failure. All the data clearly shows that the promises made simply were not kept. During the eight years of Bill Clinton's administration we created approximately 22,000,000 private-sector jobs. During the eight years that followed under George W. Bush we created a net of 1 million new private-sector jobs. When George Bush left office we were losing in excess of 700,000 jobs per month. As soon as he impact of the Obama stimulus package began to take effect we reversed the job loss and took it from a 700,000 loss per month to an average gain of about 200,000 jobs per month. We have added 8.9 million private sector jobs through April 2014 (Source-Bureau of Labor Statistics).

Today, given the fact that conservatives continue to hold on to the discredited supply-side economics that has failed this country on three separate occasions in the last 34 years, we continue to run annual budget deficit of about $650 billion per year. Thus every two years will add another $1.3 trillion to the national debt simply because of the refusal of the conservative members of Congress to recognize the impact of their policies and admit that we need to return to a tax burden that will enable us to pay our bills. The last two budgets passed by the

Republican House are a continuation of the supply-side economics that failed our country over and over again. Both of the Ryan budgets that passed the House would cut spending at a time when we are trying to stimulate the economy and give even greater tax cuts to the wealthiest Americans. Thus the conservatives have learned absolutely nothing from the experiences of 1981, 2001 and 2003. They make believe the near depression that came to a head in September 2008 is somehow a "miraculous conception" for which they have no responsibility. **Truly the policy of the conservatives to again and again to cut taxes for the wealthy in this country with the promise that it will benefit the country and balance the budget is insanity.**

Another of the conservative promises is that less regulation will result in higher growth and economic benefits to all Americans. Conservatives promised this would stimulate the growth of small business and help the middle class obtain living wage jobs. Conservatives argue the way to prosperity is to let the free market operate with little or no federal regulation so that they can unleash the entrepreneurial spirit that will produce a better life for all.

Let's take a look at what has taken place when we have allowed the wealthy and powerful to operate with little or no regulation or control. During the Golden age at the turn-of-the-century we saw the robber barons operate in a ruthless manner to the detriment of millions and millions of the average Americans. We saw country moving toward an oligarchy in which a handful of people were able to control the elected officials and pass laws that benefited themselves at the expense of others.

During the 1920s we had the same concept under Coolidge and Hoover that allowed the free market to operate virtually unfettered and with little regulation. We saw banks act in ways that were irresponsible. We allowed speculation on the securities market that produced a level of greed that was a kin to gambling. In the fall of 1929 this uncontrolled and unbridled greed in the securities markets produce the largest single economic catastrophe ever to befall the United States of America. The Great Depression saw the collapse first of the securities markets in the fall of 1929 and in 1933 the failure of many banks. Between these two occurrences both wealthy and not so wealthy lost most or all of their accumulated assets and wealth. Millions became dependent on the government and were reduced to utter poverty and despair.

Only through very aggressive policies were we able to slowly crawl out of the hole that was created by the Great Depression. In fact we were still in a serious recession at the onset of World War II. We finally ended the Great Depression and its devastating impact on our society due to the fact that our country became embroiled in the largest world war in the history of mankind.

Clearly the conservative promise that allowing the free market to operate with little control or regulation resulted in the disaster known as Great Depression. Following the Depression, Progressives were successful in regaining control of the government and passing laws and regulations to protect individuals and our economic system. Laws were passed to regulate the securities industries as well as the banks. These laws recognized that we could not allow the banks, stock market and big business to operate as the conservatives supported with little regulation or control.

Following the Second World War this country grew at a substantial rate and became the most powerful economic country the earth has ever seen. We had periods of economic slowdowns which we term business cycles and we had periods when inflation and economic stagnation did impact our country. However nothing close to the Great Depression was experienced after the Second World War. During the Eisenhower administration we began investing in the infrastructure with the interstate highway system. This was in addition to the infrastructure we built as part of the recovery from the Great Depression. All of this investment created jobs and produced long-term infrastructure that was needed for our country to grow and for our population to enjoy their leisure activities.

During the 1960s we embarked on the space program another investment which produced significant innovations that enabled companies to make new products and prosper. This continued up until the early 1980s when we began to again develop large deficits and cut spending especially on the military which had been part of the stimulus to keep the economy growing. During the period of the 70s and 80s we added very little to our infrastructure. We in fact began using up the infrastructure that we had previously built.

During the 1990s we enjoyed a period where there were no major military conflicts and we moved, for the first time in decades, toward a balanced budget. During the eight years President Clinton was in office our country saw both the wealthy and the middle class prosper. Unemployment was relatively low and we created 22 million private-sector jobs between 1992 and 2000 per the Bureau of Labor Statistics. In 2001 with the election of George W. Bush as president and the Republican controlled Congress the policies of the United States changed drastically. Regulation was relaxed and taxes were cut. The deficit ballooned and the stock market went from 14,000 in 2001 to 7,000 in early 2009.

We created 9 million private sector jobs during the first six years of the Bush administration which is less than half the rate as under Clinton. Then we lost approximately 8 million of those 9 million jobs during the economic collapse that developed in the last two years Bush was in office. **The net result was that during the eight years of George W. Bush we created a net of 1 million jobs compared with the 22 million jobs created in the preceding eight years under Clinton. The Job Growth in nearly 32 years of Democratic presidents since**

Truman took office shows an additional 57.7 million. Job growth in 36 years of Republican presidents added 34.6 million. George W. Bush had 8/10 of one percent job growth. Bill Clinton 20.7% and Obama to date is at 12% or 8.9 Million jobs during the past 5 years (Source-Bureau of Labor Statistics – October 2012).

Another promise of the conservatives is that the economy, job growth and the stock market do better when we have Republican administrations with lower taxes and less regulation. Let's take a look at how past history looks during both Republican and Democratic administrations.

How the Dow Jones Industrial Average performed during various presidential administrations:

President	Party	Average change per year in DOW
Obama	D	+25.0%
Clinton	D	+16.5%
Reagan	R	+11.2%
Eisenhower	R	+10.2%
GHWB	R	+10.7%
Truman	D	+9.4%
FDR	D	+8.0%
Ford	R	+.2%
Nixon	R	+.1%
Carter	D	-1.1%
GWB	R	-2.0%
Hoover	R	-29.0%

(Source-Bloomberg)

Percent change of GDP growth year-to-year (Based on current dollars)

Year		Percent	President	Year		Percent	President
1930	-	11.9%	Hoover	1953	+	6.0%	Eisenhower
1931	-	16.0%		1954	+	.4%	
1932	-	23.1%		1955	+	9.0%	
1933	-	4.0%	FDR	1956	+	5.6%	
1934	+	16.9%		1957	+	5.5%	

1935	+	11.5%		1958	+	1.5%	
1936	+	14.3%		1959	+	8.4%	
1937	+	9.6%		1960	+	4.0%	Kennedy/Johnson
1938	-	6.1%		1961	+	3.7%	
1939	+	7.0%		1962	+	7.4%	
1940	+	10.1%		1963	+	5.5%	
1941	+	25.7%		1964	+	7.4%	Johnson
1942	+	28.3%		1965	+	8.4%	
1943	+	22.4%		1966	+	9.6%	
1944	+	10.5%		1967	+	5.7%	
1945	+	1.6%	Truman	1968	+	9.4%	Nixon
1946	-	.2%		1969	+	8.2%	
1947	+	9.7%		1970	+	5.5%	
1948	+	9.9%		1971	+	8.5%	
1949	-	.7%		1972	+	9.8%	Nixon/Ford
1950	+	10%		1973	+	11.4%	
1951	+	15.7%		1974	+	8.4%	
1952	+	5.9%		1975	+	9.0%	
1976	+	11,2%	Carter	2000	+	6.5%	
1977	+	11.1%		2001	+	3.3%	
1978	+	13.0%		2002	+	3.3%	
1979	+	11.7%		2003	+	4.8%	
1980	+	8.8%	Reagan	2004	+	6.6%	GWB
1981	+	12.2%		2005	+	6.7%	
1982	+	4.2%		2006	+	5.8%	
1983	+	8.8%		2007	+	4.5%	
1984	+	11.1%		2008	+	1.7%	
1985	+	7.6%		2009	-	2.1%	Obama
1986	+	5.6%		2010	+	3.7%	
1987	+	6.1%		2011	+	3.8	
1988	+	7.9%	GHWB	2012	+	4.6%	Obama
1989	+	7.7%		2013	+	3.4%	
1990	+	5.7%					
1991	+	3.3%					
1992	+	5.9%	CLINTON				
1993	+	5.2%					
1994	+	6.3%					
1995	+	4.9%					
1996	+	5.7%	CLINTON				
1997	+	6.3%					
1998	+	5.6%					
1999	+	6.3%					

Source-OMB Historical Table 2.3

Pete Souza ; http://en.wikipedia.org/wiki/File:Obama_
signs_health_care-20100323.jpg

The above data on the stock market performance, job creation and growth in the Gross Domestic Product (GDP) clearly show that the promise that business and the economy grows better under a Republican administration again is a promise not kept. In fact, our country has done significantly better from an economic and business perspective during Democratic administrations.

How many times will the conservatives repeat the claim that lower taxes on the wealthy create jobs and economic growth? No matter how many times they tell us that business does better during Republican administrations with less regulation and lower taxes we see from the above data this claim is untrue. Again how many times will we have to accept the promises of a better tomorrow if only we adopt conservative policies?

Another very important example of the way the conservative promises have been unfulfilled is with the mortgage crisis that became evident beginning in 2007. This concept the conservatives hold is that we should allow business to operate with little or no oversight or regulation for they know best. This concept that the least government is the best government has brought our country to the economic abyss in 1929 and again 2008.

This idea allowed the mortgage crisis to develop and threaten the entire economy of this country and the world. What we saw in the past was mortgage creation by the banks that held them and assumed the risk when mortgage holders failed to make the required payments. When this was the case there was some self policing by the banks because they had their money at risk. Over the past 20 to 30 years there has been a change in the way mortgages are created in the United States. Mortgage brokers create the mortgage for the express purpose of resale and do not hold a mortgage or take onto themselves any risk of default. In addition the amount that the mortgage originators make is dependent on the size of the mortgage. A mortgage of $300,000 pays twice commission as a mortgage of $150,000. What we have is the Fox in the Hen House without any effective government regulation. These mortgage originators were free to operate in a way that resulted in the creation of millions of unsound mortgages just so they could make outrageous profits.

We have some conservatives trying to lay the blame on the government's encouragement for people to own homes. The Dodd / Frank laws are cited as having created the mortgage crisis when in fact nothing could be further from the truth. Homeownership is a driving force in our economy. **There is nothing more important to the economic welfare and the growth of our country then homeownership by people who can actually afford the home.** Dodd/ Frank did not encourage mortgages that were unsound; they encouraged homeownership by people who were able to pay for their home and mortgage. It was the greedy mortgage originators that created unsound mortgages simply to make a bigger profit with no effective government oversight or regulation which was in keeping with the conservative agenda.

There were two types of mortgages that created our problems. One type of mortgage is called liar loans or "no doc" loans. Almost anyone was able to obtain a mortgage if they had 20% of the purchase price without any proof that they could afford to make the mortgage payments. As the price of homes began to fall 40-50%, the 20% down was no protection for the owner of the "no-doc" mortgages. The second type of problem mortgage that was developed by the mortgage origination industry was called designer mortgages. These were mortgages that in the initial few years had payments were artificially low and individuals were qualified only on the lowest payment for the first few years of the mortgage. In many cases within two or three years the monthly mortgage payment doubled and in some cases at the end of five years the payments increased another 50%. It was not unusual to have $1,000 payment go to $2,000 at the end of three years and then to $3,000 at the end of the fifth year of the mortgage (Source-Pace Law Review, Vol 30, Fall 2009).

The result of these loans was obvious. Millions of people were unable to afford the increased payments on these mortgages and they began to go into default. These unsound mortgages for the most part were created from 2002 through 2006. They were not the result of encouraging people to buy homes. It was the result of not regulating the mortgage origination companies and allowing them to operate simply to make the most profit that they can possibly make even though they were creating unsound mortgages in the process. These unsound mortgages were bundled with conventional mortgages and rated by companies like Standard & Poor and Moody who found that they could make billions in fees from the ratings. Many of the bundles of mortgages were rated as sound when in fact many of the mortgages within those bundles were unsound. Again there was little or no regulation on how these mortgage bundles were rated.

These bundles were then resold in the secondary market principally through Fannie Mae and Freddie Mac and here again the conservative principles were clearly in play because there was little or no regulation on what types of mortgages these repurchasers could buy. If they had been restricted to repurchase loans that were qualified on a conventional basis for the entire period of mortgage payments i.e. the $1,000, $ 2,000 or $3,000 payments, these unsound designer mortgages would not have been created. If the mortgage originators had been unable to sell the unsound mortgages they had created, they would have been forced to take on the risk from default. This would have prevented mortgage originators from creating these unsound mortgages.

Finally some enterprising insurance companies like AIG decided that they could make hundreds of billions of dollars by selling a thing called a Credit Default Swaps. These Ponzi schemes were not designed to protecting the banks but simply to make huge profits for the companies selling these worthless promises. Credit default swaps were sold to reimburse a bank holding a bad mortgage should they fail. They were written in such a way to avoid being construed as insurance and Congress was prevented from either regulating them through the SEC or even having any oversight into this entire market because of a conservative amendment tacked on to a 2000 Bill (Source-www.rkmc.com-Richard R Zabel).

Here we have an example not only of failing to control or regulate this Ponzi scheme but the government actually was prevented from doing anything including oversight so companies like AIG could operate without interference. When mortgages began to fail by the hundreds of thousands and AIG was asked to reimburse the mortgage holders they were placed into a position of jeopardy that could've destroyed AIG.

At that time AIG insured all types of risks for most of the Fortune 500 corporations in the United States.

All of this is a perfect example of the failure of the conservative promise that we should allow business to act by itself and without government regulation. Not only did the conservative promise fail but that failure jeopardized the entire economic structure of the United States. It took the bailout of the banks and AIG as well as very aggressive action by the Federal Reserve and FDIC to prevent this country from falling into another Great Depression simply because we allowed mortgage originators rating companies mortgagors repurchases' and insurance companies to act in ways that were irresponsible and refused to establish effective regulation and oversight.

We constantly hear from the conservatives that the federal bureaucracy is ever-expanding and that big government is bad for the American taxpayer and the economy. In part this is an example not so much of a failed promise of a blatant untruth. The fact of the matter is that the employment and the size of government in absolute numbers is the lowest that is been in 47 years. We have to go back to 1966 to find a smaller federal government. **Today federal workers constitute 2% of the nation's total labor force in 1966 federal employees accounted for 4.3% of the American workforce. Despite the facts, the conservatives continue to complain about big government which is simply a lie.**

Federal **Government workers (in thousands) from the Office of Personnel Management:**

Year	Executive Branch	Military	Legislative	Total
1966	2,726	3,129	33	**5,888**
1980	2,821	2,090	55	**4,965**

1992	3,017	1,848	66	**4,931**
2000	2,639	1,426	63	**4,129**
2008	2,692	1,450	64	**4,206**
2013	2,721	1,400	65	**4,186**

What the conservatives are saying is we can prove that government is bigger because it's spending more. This is all part of their philosophy to cut government spending whenever possible. The truth of the matter is that much of the federal budget is subject to inflation. Every one of the 2.7 million federal workers gets a raise each year in addition to the 1.4 million military. Federal retirees both civilian and military get a Cost of Living Allowance (COLA) which increases the spending at the federal government level. Everything the government buys goes up in price whether it is for food, clothing, and gasoline. When the government contracts for work the cost of inflation to contractors drives up the cost of the federal government. When in 2007-2008 we had a loss of 8 million jobs and people began drawing unemployment and food stamps federal spending went up. That did not mean that the size of government increased. It simply means that the number of dollars our government had to spend to deal with the economic disaster increased.

This conservative concept that big government is bad does dovetail into another broken conservative promise that it's good to cut the budget and that will help our economy. The truth of the matter is that the spending cuts since 2011 have cost 1 million government jobs per the CBO. That means that those million people and their families cut their spending that does harm to the economy. Many of these government workers that lost their jobs started drawing unemployment which increased federal spending. This idea that government spending does not create jobs and does not stimulate the economy is simply a broken promise and a lie being told to us by the conservatives.

When the federal government spends a dollar it generally goes to private contractors to buy things or provide services. That money turns into salary wages and profits. It's as if the conservatives want us to believe every time the government spends a dollar it goes into the black hole of Calcutta. When the government spends money the multiplier effect produces economic growth jobs profits and economic well-being. **We should not pay for the added spending by increasing our debt and the interest to service that debt. The solution is to increase our tax revenue so as we can "pay as we go" for the things that we need and for the investments to help our country grow. We do that by asking those making huge sums of money to pay more and return to the pre-2000 tax rates and eliminate or minimize the loopholes which enable the wealthy to avoid paying their fair share of taxes.** When you have someone like Mitt Romney with a $20 Million dollar annual income paying only 14% we see a person who in not meeting his responsibility to our country.

Despite the fact conservatives claim we need to create more jobs their budget policies are producing the exact opposite result and they are therefore not keeping the promise that spending cuts will help our economy.

While the conservatives complain that job growth has not been rapid enough they have refused to approve the jobs bill President Obama proposed more than two years ago. According to the CBO, this jobs bill which is primarily infrastructure repair would've added 2 million living wage private sector jobs. **Thus the promise that spending cuts and their refusal to invest in our country is good for the country is incorrect.** The conservative refusal to provide added government spending for police, firefighters, teachers and infrastructure repair has cost at least 3 million jobs per the Congressional Budget Office (CBO). In addition, their refusal to extend the unemployment benefits according to the CBO will cost another 330,000 jobs.

The list goes on which clearly demonstrates over and over again the conservative dogma and policies that they repeat over and over again are not keeping the promise of a better life for the majority of Americans. To the contrary, we would be further down the pike to a balanced budget with 3 million more people working and corporations would have the added profits from all the infrastructure repairs. All this would increase the tax revenue and reduce the annual budget deficit.

Even if the infrastructure repairs were not needed to create jobs they are needed to keep in repair things that we use every day in both our commercial and personal lives. At the present time there are approximately 63,000 bridges that desperately need repair. As of October 2014 if Congress does not act there will be no money to continue road repair in the United States. The conservatives' refusal to invest in our country and repair our infrastructure carried to extreme will bring us huge economic problems in the future. In addition to the 63,000 bridges that need repair, we have more than 4,000 dams in need of work. We have antiquated and ineffective power transmission systems. Many of our sewer and water systems in our major cities are in excess of 100 years old. Rather than ask the wealthy to pay higher taxes and invest that money to rebuild our infrastructure, the conservatives insist that government spending is not necessary and would not create jobs. Even if the spending on our infrastructure didn't create a single new job the fact is our infrastructure needs to be repaired.

There is no part of the conservative agenda that is moving this country forward to create jobs, increase GDP growth or help the middle class in our country. The policies they support and have proposed for the future, as reflected in the last two budgets that passed the House of

Representatives, benefit only the wealthy while cutting the safety net for the people in need. The top 10% have done well over the last 10 to 12 years and the top 5% extremely well. The increase in wealth of the top 1% is off the scale. Despite the growth that we have seen for the very wealthy in our country, we still have conservative multibillionaire's complaining about the role of government and the Obama policies.

Some very pointed examples of wealthy conservatives and their distorted view of the federal government include Sheldon Adelson, CEO of Las Vegas Sands Corporation. Mr. Adelson reportedly had a net worth when President Obama took office of approximately $3 billion. Today he is reportedly worth somewhere in the neighborhood of $37 billion. Despite this fact, he complains bitterly about government regulation and the policies of Barack Obama. He is a man that wants the federal government to regulate online gambling to help protect his casino empire. His net worth reportedly has gone up approximately 13 times yet he complains about the way government prevents business from prospering and growing.

Another example are the Koch brothers who also bitterly complain about President Obama and his progressive policies. Their net worth reportedly went from $38 billion when President Obama took office to $77 billion today. These two brothers spent over $400 million in the last presidential election to defeat President Obama's reelection.

Yet a third conservative billionaire who constantly blasts President Obama and his policies is Kenneth Langdon, cofounder of Home Depot. Here is another example of a man whose net worth has reportedly doubled since President Obama took office.

All of these and other conservative billionaires have very short memories. **These wealthy conservatives as well as all other Americans should think back to September 2008 and the near Depression that resulted after eight years of conservative control. The fall** of 2008 was a kin to the fall of 1929. Only because of the very aggressive action to approve TARP, the aggressive action of the Federal Reserve and the FDIC as well as the stimulus package did we avoid another great depression.

Chapter 4

Broken Promises—Social Issues

Some of the most contentious policies of the conservatives revolve around social issues. The attempts to restrict birth control to women of limited means by defunding Planned Parenthood add to unwanted pregnancies. Conservatives contend that choice should be made by the conservatives not by individual women with respect to abortion. The defunding of programs to help low income women with preventative health screening increases health care costs in the future.

We see continued efforts by conservatives to reduce health care for the poor. In almost 30 states Republican governors are refusing to expand the Medicaid coverage provided in the Affordable Healthcare Act to help millions of low income Americans to have health coverage. We see the cuts to the food stamp program which is designed to help the poorest of the poor, as well as children and women of childbearing age. We see the refusal of the conservatives to extend unemployment benefits even though there are not enough jobs to employ the millions of people that lost their ability to make a living as a result of the near depression handed us by the conservatives and George W. Bush. We have continued resistance to provide Life, Liberty and the Pursuit of happiness to poor and many middle class Americans.

One of the most onerous cuts that conservatives have made in their last two budgets passed by the House of Representatives are those for food stamps (CHIP). Almost every major church in the United States has taken the position that these cuts are not justified and that they will harm the poorest of the poor including children, seniors and the disabled. One grassroots effort to try and defeat Paul Ryan's food stamp cuts is headed by Sister Simone Campbell. She is operating a thing called, "A nun on the bus". Her movement stresses that our policies must include all not just some Americans. She has been very effective in opposing the drastic spending cuts to the social network that Paul Ryan and the conservatives have championed in the House of Representatives. **It is ironic that Paul Ryan who was a Roman Catholic is insisting on cuts for the most needy in our country while proposing yet even more tax cuts for the wealthiest in America. At least on these issues Paul Ryan has made a very clear choice to put his conservative policies above the teachings of his religion.**

Many of the social positions taken by conservatives express the feeling that many of these people are **on** the dole and that they really don't need the help. There is no question we have some people "game the system" and should not be receiving assistance or help at taxpayer expense. We have a responsibility as a society to both weed out those who should not be receiving help because they are capable of helping themselves while at the same time helping those that through no fault of their own need help either for an interim period or in the case of the disabled for a lifetime. Making believe that each and every person without a job can fix their problem by starting a small business or going back to school is another concept conservatives push and is another broken promise to the poor in our country. These options are solutions for some but not for many unemployed.

One of the most fundamental problems and one that has a very real economic consequence is the refusal to approve an increased to the minimum wage. No one should be paid so little that even though they work they cannot afford to live on their income. That is exactly the situation millions of workers are in today with the minimum wage of $7.25 per hour. **To just offset the impact of inflation, the minimum wage should be $10.60 per hour. Thus raising the minimum wage to $10.60 is not increasing it but merely offsetting the impact of inflation (Source-www.pewresearch.org).**

If we were to raise the minimum wage, we would provide millions of Americans billions of dollars more to spend which helps the economy. Every added dollar that someone making minimum wage would receive as an increase would be spent. This would be an immediately benefit the overall economy of our country. The conservative argument that small businesses cannot afford to pay higher wages is offset by the fact that many of the corporations paying minimum wage are the fast food industry and the banks that can well afford to increase the minimum wage.

For the small businesses that simply cannot afford to pay a reasonable wage to the workers in their company should not be in business. To continue to have a business depend on paying non living wages so they can exist is simply not only morally wrong but is financially harming the economy of this country. **There is a concept called the" marginal propensity to consume". This is the concept that has been proven over and over again that for a lower income people the next dollar they receive will be spent. The higher your income the less of the next dollar that you receive will be spent. Thus the conservative idea of granting tax cuts to the rich means that very little if any**

of that additional money given to the wealthy is spent whereas help for a low income Americans by raising the minimum wage, increasing food stamps, extending unemployment or helping the disabled is immediately spent and benefits our economy.

The position taken by the conservatives on social issues has failed to deal with our country's needs in very real ways. It is difficult to argue that we should turn our backs on people who simply need help in order to survive. It is hard to justify allowing the top few percent to become more wealthy at the rate they have been and ignore the most basic needs of people that simply have no place else to turn. The concept that conservatives have that this problem should be handled by churches and charities is a copout of our responsibility as a country to help those that need help. Yes churches and charities provide enormous benefit to people in need. But the reality is that the needs of the poor and disabled today are far greater than can be satisfied by all the churches and all the charities in our great nation. How are those with nothing to enjoy, Life, Liberty, and the Pursuit of Happiness?

The resistance of the conservatives to grant the same rights to gays as to heterosexuals is also very difficult to justify. Conservatives argue we must return to the concepts of our Founding Fathers which include providing everyone with the ability to enjoy Life, Liberty, and the Pursuit of Happiness. Given the conservative position on gay marriage how are those whose sexual orientation is different, to have those basic rights? It does not seem as if the conservatives really mean what they say when they claim that we should return to our roots and honor the covenants that our Founding Fathers intended for this country when they oppose gay marriage.

Many conservatives oppose choice for women and want to make abortion illegal. They also at the same time do not want to provide poor women with family planning and birth control. These two positions are diametrically opposed for if we provide family planning and birth control to low income women we reduce the possibility of unwanted pregnancies and abortions. Each person is entitled to their own opinion as to whether or not abortion should be legal. I for one do not believe it is the right alternative to be used as birth control. At the same time, the right to choose, which was granted to human kind by God is not something that the conservatives should be legislating away.

For those who are so adamantly opposed to any form of abortion I suggest that they redouble their efforts to help women with family planning and provide alternatives for unwanted pregnancy such as adoption. There is nothing wrong with trying to help women make choices that avoid abortion as a means of dealing with an unwanted pregnancy. In fact there is everything right and moral with those efforts. But to try and remove God-given free will, as conservatives advocate, is wrong.

One of the most important issues that conservatives have staked out is the Affordable Healthcare Act and the drive to cover most Americans with health insurance. This issue certainly could be classed as a social issue but also has economic impact as well. Whether or not the dire predictions of the conservatives will materialize is yet to be determined. Certainly by the 2016 presidential election we will have a far better idea of the overall impact that the Affordable Healthcare Act had on health coverage and health costs in the United States.

To date some of the dire predictions of the conservatives concerning the Affordable Healthcare Act have not materialized. **Conservatives promised the law would be a total failure**. So far we have seen some very real successes. We have 3 million students covered by health insurance that would not have coverage had it not been for this law. We have help for seniors to pay their prescription drug costs. We have preventive care for both seniors and women that heretofore had not been available. Restrictions have been placed on insurance companies so they cannot deny coverage because of pre-existing condition. We have ended the practice of lifetime limits as well as terminating coverage whenever an individual begins to incur large medical expenses.

The two big issues that are not clear are will we be able to cover the vast majority of those that did not have insurance prior to the Affordable Healthcare Act, and second, will health care cost be lower? To date approximately 8 million people have signed up for the coverage under the act. However unless we have significantly more people opt for coverage under the law the objective to cover 35 million Americans that did not have health insurance is still a question. Certainly if by 2016 the Affordable Healthcare Act has enabled the bulk of the uninsured to be covered and the law has made some inroads into reducing the health care cost spiral, we will have a huge conservative promise that was not kept. If the health care act does meet most of its objectives the conservatives will most likely be held to account by the voters in 2016 and beyond. Given the extent that the conservatives have gone to defeat and prevent this law from succeeding it would be difficult for voters to ignore their actions if there is a relatively high degree of success long-term of the Affordable Healthcare Act.

If it succeeds and becomes something akin to Medicare and Social Security in the mind's eye of most Americans, conservatives will refer to the act as the Affordable Healthcare Act. If the law fails to achieve its major objectives we will hear that Obamacare has failed from all conservatives.

Chapter 5

Broken Promises—Foreign policy and military issues

One of the major promises of the conservatives is that the use of military power, especially in the Middle East, will reduce the threat of further violence against the United States and help prevent another 9/11. Within the conservative movement is a group which has been dubbed the neocons (Neoconservatives) who favor using our military power to deal with most trouble spots throughout the world.

After the terrorist attack on 9/11 George W. Bush and his conservative coalition invaded Afghanistan believing that the attacks from 9/11 were planned and directed by Al Qaeda utilizing Afghanistan as a home base of operation. Most Americans agreed with Bush and the conservatives that in fact it was necessary, given the horrendous attack on the United States, that we act to neutralize and punish those responsible for that unprovoked attack on our homeland. Very close to the same time, George W. Bush decided it was time to invade Iraq which had absolutely nothing to do with 9/11 or with the Al Qaeda factions operating within Afghanistan. As a result of invading Iraq, the Afghan war was put on the back burner and was denied the necessary military assets to prosecute that war. The impact of that decision was to take a war that should have lasted two years and drag it out for almost 11 years.

We can write volumes as to the efficacy of invading Iraq. It is now clear that Bush at the time he choose to invade Iraq had the intelligence that clearly documented the fact that Saddam Hussein had no weapons of mass distraction. In addition, a Pentagon study in December prior to the invasion determined that Saddam Hussein was no military threat to the United States. That analysis said he was only able to conduct militarily operations within the central part of Iraq itself. Despite that George W. Bush invaded Iraq as if Iraq were a threat to the United States with the promise that he would plant the "tree of democracy" in the Middle East and reduce the threat from terrorist attacks in the future (Source-Pentagon Assessment of Iraq Military- December 2002).

More than 10 years later almost every intelligence estimate clearly shows that the invasion of Iraq and the war in Afghanistan has not fundamentally changed the threat to our country posed by the militant Islamic factions. The conservatives will cite the fact that we have not been attacked again like we were on 9/11 as proof that their promise has been kept.

The reason we have not been attacked again is because of the defensive measures that we have taken to protect our country. The invasion of Iraq and Afghanistan created more enemies for the United States and it is believed that there is a greater risk today from attack then prior to 9/11, 2001. Therefore the conservative promise of invading Iraq and Afghanistan would significantly reduce the threat to our country in the future has simply not been achieved.

Not only has this conservative promise not been kept but the cost to our country in both human and financial resources is staggering. We had 4,488 US service personnel killed directly in Iraq. We have more than 2,000 more killed in Afghanistan. We had 32,223 troops directly injured in Iraq and that figure does not include another hundred thousand that are most likely suffered from PTSD.

The CBO has documented that we have spent directly on the wars in Iraq and Afghanistan $1.7 trillion. This figure does not include the cost of the equipment that was destroyed nor does it include the cost of the interest that this war has added to our national debt. It does not include an estimated $754 billion that we will spend through the VA over the next 30 to 40 years to deal with the injuries created in these two wars. In 2002, George W. Bush and his conservative cohorts including Dick Cheney estimated the cost of the Iraq war would be in the $50-$60 billion range. There are a number of studies that have tried to develop a comprehensively estimate of the cost of the Iraq and Afghan wars. A Brown University study estimates that the cost will be $3.2-$4 trillion. The Brookings Institute has done a study which shows the cost could be as high as $6 trillion when you consider interest that was added to the debt, VA costs, equipment repair and replacement as well as the direct expense incurred during the fighting in Iraq and Afghanistan.

Whether you choose the $4 trillion or the $6 trillion estimate, the cost to fulfill this promise of greater stability by invading Iraq and Afghanistan is horrendous. We listen to the conservatives complain about spending and that we need to cut the budget in ways that harm poorest and most needy in our country. We can grant trillions of dollars of tax cuts to the wealthiest people in our nation while we spent $4 to 6 trillion to keep a promise that was simply not kept. After all of that, we still have factions within the conservative movement today who immediately want to use, either directly or indirectly, our military to affect change throughout the world.

Several books have been written about the hubris of the United States thinking that it can change the history of the thousand years or eliminate the animosity between religious factions and change the basic structure of governance in countries like Afghanistan, Iraq, Iran, Syria and Pakistan. The truth of the matter is we cannot materially change a thousand years of history that are responsible for the tensions that exist in the Middle East and the Muslim world. Repeating the mistakes that we made in Afghanistan and Iraq to satisfy the ill-conceived policies of the conservative neocons is unthinkable.

Just imagine what our country could have done with the $4-$6 trillion wasted on the two Bush wars. How many bridges could we have repaired? How many students could we have sent to college? How many people could we have helped refinance their mortgages so they do not lose their homes? How long could we have extended unemployment benefits? How many people could we have fed? Every one of these alternate expenditures would have produced positive results. It would have created Jobs, reduce suffering, educated the future generation and helped millions to remain in their homes. What do we have to show from spending of $4-$6 trillion in Iraq and Afghanistan? We have a greater risk of future terrorist attack and the death of 6,500 of our military? Is it worth another hundred thousand that will suffer for many years in the future from the physical and mental injuries incurred fighting those two wars? Although there are many that would agree that the initial attack against Afghanistan was justified when we diverted our attention to get involved with Iraq we took a war that should have lasted two years turned it into an 11 year war, the longest in our history. We could have done what was needed to be done in Afghanistan with a fraction of the cost both in dollars and lives had we not invaded Iraq.

The Bush wars are one of the most reprehensible broken promises of the conservatives. We need to be very careful in the future in our use of military power to address terrorism and other areas of unrest throughout the world. A massive invasion with hundreds of thousands of troops rarely is necessary to achieve the desired result. What we are seeing today is more surgical approach whereby we try and punish or eliminate directly the elements responsible without committing huge numbers of troops for long periods of time which cause, death, injuries and untold amount of added spending. It does not seem to matter to those that drink the conservative Kool-Aid as to the failure that is evident by our invasion of Iraq and Afghanistan. They continue to seek the use of our military in almost every conceivable situation that develops.

Chapter 6

Why must the American voter abandon the conservatives?

There are two principal reasons the American voter must abandon the conservatives beginning in 2014.

First the conservative promises have not been kept. As demonstrated in the preceding pages, with hard data and facts, what the Conservatives have promised and what they have delivered are two very different things. **To continue to repeat over and over again the same conservative policies and expect a different result is clearly as Albert Einstein said the definition of insanity.**

The second reason why voters must reject the conservatives is that the vast majority of Americans simply do not support the conservative agenda to deal with the major issues that face our country. These issues are such that they must be dealt with for our country to prosper and continue to be strong both economically and militarily. If we are to deliver the promises of Life, Liberty, and the Pursuit of Happiness we must deal with things like the minimum wage, the distribution of wealth, the ability for students to obtain the education and training needed to secure employment in the 21st century, to rebuild and repair the infrastructure that is absolutely essential for both commerce and for our daily lives, to invest in research from which the new products and services of the 21st and 22nd centuries will evolve. We must balance our budget and begin repaying a debt before it destroys our economy. **Simply saying NO or trying to prevent solutions to these issues is not the answer and is dangerous to the future of our country.**

Let's take a look at the major issues that we face and the conservative solution to each issue.

Minimum Wage-The most recent poll shows 69% of Americans support increasing the Minimum wage. Conservatives are preventing that from taking place.

Funding Social Security-There is no question Social Security has a funding problem that must be addressed. The conservatives want to privatize Social Security that will subject it to the risks of the stock market and do absolutely nothing to deal with the funding shortfall that exists given the baby boomers over the next 50 to 60 years. **As much as 80% of the American people simply do not want to privatize Social Security.** Conservatives continue to try and change the very structure of Social Security even though most Republicans as well as most Americans simply do not agree with the policy.

Funding Medicare-The question of the solvency of Medicare long-term is a given. We must find solutions to help keep the promise of health care after retirement for our American population. The conservatives want to convert the current system to a voucher plan which provides a given amount to each senior with which they can then attempt to purchase insurance to cover their health needs during retirement. This approach would transfer the cost problem to the retired and produce hardship on millions and millions of retired Americans. **Again as much as 80% of the American people do not agree with the conservative**

way of fixing Medicare even though they wanted it to remain solvent.

Tax cuts for the wealthiest Americans-conservatives continue to push for more and more tax cuts for the wealthiest Americans. Case in point are the last two budgets the House of Representatives passed which would lower taxes for the wealthy and aggravate the deficit. The CBO has estimated that the Ryan budgets will increase the deficit. Nevertheless, conservatives push ahead with their plans to cut help for those at the bottom and give more to those at the top. **The majority of voters believe the wealthy should pay more not less of their income in taxes.**

Background checks for gun purchases-As many as 90% of Americans favor background checks before anyone can purchase a firearm. Despite this fact conservatives have managed to block legislation that would require background checks before the purchase of firearms.

Funding cuts of social programs-Poll after poll shows that most Americans do not want to turn their backs on the poor, disabled or the unemployed. At the same time most taxpayers do not want to support people who are able to work. However, the slash and burn approach taken by the conservatives is not acceptable to the majority of Americans. A very real inconsistency in the conservative policy of cutting the budget and reducing fraud is they have cut auditors needed to help control fraud. The spending cuts that began in 2011 have reduced the number of auditors in all agencies of the federal government. You do not lower fraud by cutting those charged with preventing fraud (Source- AP 4/13/2014).

Tax Reform-There is a lot of complaining about our income tax system but no action to reform it. The law is full of loopholes that are designed to reduce or eliminate taxes for the very wealthy. The Bush tax cuts lowered the tax rates mostly for wealthier individuals. He kept the loopholes that enable people like Mitt Romney to only pay 14% tax in federal income tax while his secretary pays 25% tax. We constantly hear the conservatives complain about high taxes in the United States. The truth is, taxes are at an 80 year low. Tax freedom day which is intended to measure the date when we finish paying all taxes—federal, state and local for the year has gone from May 1, in 2000 to April 21st in 2014. That clearly demonstrating that the total tax burden in the United States has dropped since 2000 (Source-www.taxfoundation.org).

When we look at our tax burden compared with the other industrialized nations we find the United States ranks third from the bottom. In a 2010 study done by the Organization of Economic Cooperation and Development (OECD) found the United States had a total tax burden federal, state and local of 24.5% of GDP. This compares with 40 to 45% of GDP in most of the European countries.

The CBO reported that the tax burden from just the federal income tax was at 21% of GDP in 2000 when we had a balanced budget. In 2013 the federal income tax is 15.5% of GDP. The impact of reducing the income tax revenue from 21% of GDP to 15.5% of GDP is more than an $800 billion per year loss in revenue. When you add the lost revenue because of the loopholes and the tax cheats there is no doubt why this country is running a budget deficit.

Immigration reform-The majority of Americans do not want to deport 11 million people who have not entered our country legally. Most Americans recognize that there needs to be a solution to this problem and that there should be some mechanism for those who want to remain here to do so legally. But here again even though we have had a comprehensive measure to deal with immigration pass the Senate, conservatives in the House refuse to allow this bill to come to a vote. Most Americans do not support what the conservatives are doing by only allowing bills to come to a vote when Republicans believe they have the votes to get their way on a Bill. Nor do most people support the conservative tactic of using the filibuster in the Senate to again prevent a vote. The filibuster has been used over 450 times since President Obama took office. Preventing a vote in either the House or the Senate does not allow either chamber to function as the Constitution intended. The purpose of these two parts of the legislative branch was to vote and render their decision on proposed legislation. **When conservatives prevent a vote, they shelter their members from going on record to either support or oppose the measure in question. This shelters the Congressperson or Senator from the scrutiny of the electorate.**

Rebuilding the infrastructure-Despite the fact that everyone understands we need safe highways, bridges and dams as well as an effective electrical grid the conservatives have repeatedly prevented the repair and maintenance of these essential elements. Two years ago President Obama proposed a Bill to help create jobs and rebuild our infrastructure. Even if we did not need the jobs that the infrastructure repair will create the fact of the matter is for both our business and personal use we must have a viable infrastructure. All the estimates that the engineers have made document that we have trillions of dollars in needed repairs that are not being done because the conservatives will not approve the spending (Source-American Society of Civil Engineers Report 2013). **The Federal gas tax revenue has been falling due to the increase in vehicle fuel-efficiency. Add to this the increase in the cost of asphalt as well as road construction and the result is the Highway Trust Fund will be insolvent by October 1, 2014 unless Congress acts. Conservatives have blocked added funding for highway construction and have no answers when bridges and other infrastructure fail.**

We need to change the gasoline tax system from a fixed per gallon tax to one that is adjusted each year for increased road construction costs and fuel-efficiency growth.

Our parents and grandparents spent the money to build the infrastructure so that we could prosper as a nation. The conservatives simply ignore the fact that our bridges dams and roads are getting older and must be repaired. We need to obtain the resources needed to make these repairs by having the wealthy in our country pay more in taxes. We simply cannot afford to make the necessary repairs and add it to the national debt.

The United States is at a crossroads. We cannot simply ignore the major issues we face because of their magnitude and impact on our country and each of our lives. **When you look at the conservative agenda you will see it has either created the problem or enabled the problem to develop.** Two of the best examples of this are the increase in the National Debt from $900 billion in 1980 to $17.5 trillion in 2014. The tax and spend policies of Reagan and George W. Bush are responsible for most of the increase the national debt. Most recently we started with a balanced budget (2000) and reduced the federal revenue by 30% with the Bush tax cuts and then increase spending by 10% to pay the added cost of two Bush wars. The result was a huge deficit. This is precisely what we did in 2001-2003 despite the fact that the very same conservative policy, employed in 1981, produced the very same increase in the deficit.

The common thread that runs through the conservative agenda is repeated over and over again. Conservatives ignore the facts to justify an ideology that simply doesn't work. Everything from the budget to global warming demonstrates the fact that conservatives are more like religious zealots then informed people. We have 98% of world scientists acknowledge that global warming is taking place.

They have measured the increase in ocean temperature. They have documented that the level of the oceans have risen approximately a foot. We have satellite images that prove the polar caps are melting and we measured the increased acidity of the ocean from the carbon dioxide that we are putting into the atmosphere by burning fossil fuels. Increasing the Ph of the oceans is killing the coral and many types of marine life TODAY. Despite all of this we have some conservatives that will not even acknowledge there is global warming.

The comments made by Senator Marco Rubio Sunday, May 11, 2014 on ABC's *This Week* are a perfect example of conservatives ignoring reality. Senator Rubio said "I don't agree with the notion that some are putting out there, including scientists, that somehow there are actions we can take today that would actually have an impact on what's happening in our climate" He then blasted President Obama as "Commander-in-chief, not a meteorologist" What credentials does Senator Rubio have as a meteorologist? **He went on to say, "And I do not believe the laws (scientists) propose we pass will do anything about it, except it will destroy our economy". What does Senator Rubio think loosing the Gulf, Boston, New York or most of the coastal areas of Florida would do to our economy?**

It may be that global warming would occur even without the untold amounts of CO2 we are putting into the atmosphere but the issue is we are probably accelerating the global warming process. However, to deny that global warming is even taking place and do nothing is risking a global catastrophe.

Our country needs to totally reverse what began in 1981 and reemerged in 2001. If we are to prosper and hand our sons and daughters and grandchildren a vibrant free nation we need to resolve the issues we face. **It is time to rebuild and repair our infrastructure. It is time to invest in basic research. It is time to make sure that every student is**

able to get the education and training necessary so that they can be productive members of society. We need to balance our budget and begin paying down the huge debt before the interest on that debt buries us all. We need to take a look at the changing atmospheric conditions in our world and see what we can do either to slow the progress or to provide some defensive mechanisms to protect us from the rising oceans. We need to deal with the funding issues that jeopardize Social Security and Medicare. We need to get a handle on the ever-increasing costs of healthcare. We need to do a better job at increasing the minimum wage, streamline our welfare systems to help those that needed help and deny help to those who would abuse it.

All of this is going to take a joint effort between government and the private sector. We must have effective regulation and honestly look at our country and the reasons why we have the major problems that we have today. **The biggest problem with the conservatives is that they are not interested in WHY things happened because when they look at the WHY, they find that it comes directly into conflict with their philosophy and the policies.** No place is this more clear than in what caused the deficit to rise or what caused the Great Depression and a near depression 2008. **We need to have those with the resources pay more of their income not to punish the wealthy but because we need the money. We need the added money to balance our budget and make the investments in our country that are absolutely essential to ensure our future welfare.**

The American people do not want to repeat the suffering that our parents and grandparents endured in the 1929-33. Americans want to avoid the misery we endured because of the recession of 2007-2008. **The voters of this country need to recognize that the conservative agenda has not kept its promise. The conservative agenda is** primarily responsible for the deficit as well as allowing business to act without restraint which resulted in the Great Depression and the near depression that came to a head in 2008. For anyone that would like to relive these difficult periods, I suggest they support the conservatives. <u>For any American that wants to avoid another Great Depression or the economic crisis we lived through in 2008, it is time to remove the conservatives from a position of power in the House, Senate and keep them out of the White House.</u> If the Democrats are unable to control 60 votes in the Senate but get control of the House and White House, they will need to again change the Senate Rules to either make a filibuster a true filibuster by requiring the Senator to speak on the subject or by requiring only 51 votes to bring a bill to a vote in the Senate.

For any voter who is still undecided as to whether or not the conservatives deserve to remain in any position of power within the federal government consider the following. We were promised that the Iraq war would be quick, remember the "Shock and Awe", and would cost $50 to $60 billion. The Iraq and Afghan wars cost this country somewhere between $4 and $6 Trillion and lasted 11 years.

In 1980, Ronald Reagan promised that if we reduce taxes for the wealthy we would balance the budget and the benefits would trickle-down to the middle class. George W. Bush made the same promise in 2001. The bottom line is the wealth in our country is far more concentrated at the top then it has never been in the past. Middle income Americans are struggling to simply live. We have created a mountain of debt. The promises of Ronald Reagan and George W. Bush were not kept. <u>Their conservative agenda has added $16.5 trillion to the National Debt. That means each year the American taxpayer is paying between $660 and $825 billion</u>

in interest to service the increase in the debt caused by the broken conservative promises.

What is even more disturbing is what we did with that $16.5 Trillion dollars since 1981? Approximately $2 trillion was used to fight the Bush wars. The remaining $14.5 trillion was used to pay for the day to day operating costs of the United States. We did not use it to build roads, build bridges or educate our children. It was not paid to retirees for Social Security or Medicare. None of this money was used to invest in long-term infrastructure that would benefit us in the future. It would be as if in your home budget you borrowed 30% of the amount that you spent every month on food, clothing, utilities and things to simply live.

Whether the Democrats will effectively resolve all our problems we cannot be sure. However, we can be certain that if the conservatives remain in a position where they can either set policy or prevent changes in the policies we are following, our country is headed for a very serious economic and social upheaval the likes of which we have not experienced since our founding in 1776!

Conservatives are entitled to their own opinions but they are NOT entitled to their own facts!

Anyone who would like to see what it was like to live during the Great Depression or to relive the near Depression that came to a head in September 2008 should continue to support the conservatives and vote Republican in 2016 and beyond.

About the Author

Gene P. Abel is a person that is not satisfied with the status quo and has always been in the forefront of change. He was born in Allentown, Pennsylvania in 1941. Mr. Abel is from a German and Scottish heritage and was educated in the public school system. He earned a B.S. from Penn State in finance/economics and an MBA from Lehigh University. He was a distinguished military graduate and received a regular army commission as a second lieutenant in the field artillery branch of the Army in 1963. Abel served as a nuclear weapons officer in Germany and a member of the nuclear release authority that begins with the President and ended with Lt Abel. Upon the completion of his tour in Germany, he spent two years as a finance officer at Ft Lewis, Washington. After four years of active duty he accepted a reserve commission as a Captain in the Army Reserve and left active duty in 1968.

He remained in the Army Reserve until 1993 and retired at the rank of Colonel. He is a graduate of the Army War College and was awarded numerous medals including a Meritorious Service Medal on two occasions. He was promoted to Colonel after only 19 years of service and was nominated for promotion to general officer soon after completing the Army War College. However, his lack of combat service, which is most likely the result of his very sensitive assignment in nuclear weapons, prevented his promotion to the ranks of general officer. Colonel Abel's last assignment was as the Commander of the US

Army Financial Services Activity. This unit had the responsibility to the financial operations of up to 500,000 troops in time of war.

After leaving the Army, he became a financial analyst in the space and electronics industries. In 1969 he began a13 year career as a mid-level executive at the University of Pennsylvania and then at the Hahnemann Medical College and Hospital. In 1981, he was asked to return active duty to head the team redesigning the military pay system for the Army Reserve and National Guard.

In 1983, upon returning to civilian life, he became an officer of a 2-billion-dollar bank where he was in charge of the bank operations at over 50 locations. In 1985, Mr. Abel returned to education and was appointed Dean of Business Services at the Reading Area Community College. His last position was the chief operating officer for one of the largest school districts in Pennsylvania. During the more than 12 years he served as the chief operating officer of the Central Bucks School District, he built over $120 million of new schools in addition to running this rapidly growing school system.

Mr. Abel was active in politics in the 70's and served as a committee person and campaign chairman for the state legislator in his area. His biography appears in Who's Who in the World and Who's Who in Finance and he was certified for Federal Senior Executive Service positions. He has written 3 books and scores of articles that have been published throughout the country.

In 1998 he retired to Southwest Florida with Carol, his wife of 26 years. In 2006 he was president of the Cape Coral Housing, Rehabilitation and Development Corporation, a nonprofit organization that provides low-income senior housing and helps low income homeowners repair their homes. He served on the board of the Christ Lutheran Church School in Cape Coral, Florida. In 2008 his late wife Carol passed away from cancer and Mr. Abel returned to Pennsylvania.

In 2010 Mr. Abel met a Jersey girl, Susan Bittner and was married in January 2011. Susan is a Med Tech at the local hospital and they live in South Jersey with Susan's two boys. Mr. Abel currently serves on the Church Council of Apostles' Lutheran Church in Turnersville, NJ and remains engaged in politics.

Mr. Abel has three children, five stepchildren and seven grandchildren.

Sources used in "Broken promises of the Conservatives",
by Gene P. Abel

American Society of Civil Engineers
Bloomberg
Brookings Institute
Brown University
Bureau of labor statistics
Bureau of Public Debt, Department of the Treasury
Central Intelligence Agency (CIA)
Congressional Budget Office (CBO)
Department of Defense (DoD)
Harvard Business School
Institute on Taxation and Economic Policy (ITEP)
Iraq Study Group (ISG) David Kay
Martens, Pam
National Oceanic and Atmospheric Administration (NOAA)
New York Times
Office of Management and Budget (OMB)-Historical Tables
Office of Personnel Management (OPM)
Organization for Economic Cooperation and Development (OECD)
Pace Law Review
Pew Research
Philanthropy Magazine
Politico
Reprints Long Form.org
RKMC.org
Scientific American
Tax Foundation (Tax Freedom Day)
The Economist
Treasury Direct
U.S. Dept. of Commerce, Bureau of Economic Analysis

INDEX

A

ABC *This Week* 68

Abortion 21,54

Adelson, Sheldon 49

Affordable Healthcare Act. 41,51,55,56

Afghanistan war 32,57,58,59,60,61

AIG. 7,18,44,45

Al Qaeda 57

American Business 27

American Voter 27,62

Annual Budget Deficit 16, 28, 29-36,63, 67, 69, 70

Anti-Tax 30

Articles of Confederation 11

B

Bachmann, Michelle 20

Background checks 64

Balanced Budget 29,33,69

Bank Failure 8,9,10,11,37

Big Business 37

Big Government 25,45,46

Billionaires 49

Birth control 25

Bridges 48,71

Broken Promises 51

Brookings Institute 59

Brown, Scott 34

Brown University 59

Budget Deficit 28,32,33,34,35,65

Buffett, Warren 32

Bundles of Mortgages 43

Bush Administration 16

Bureau of Labor Statistics 38

Bush, George Herbert Walker 30

Bush, George W. 17,31-35,38,51,57,67,70

Bushvilles 17

Bureau of Public Debt 31

Business Cycles 37

C

Calcutta 47

Campbell, Sister Simone 52

Captains of Industry 1,4

Carnegie, Andrew 1,5

Carnegie Institute 5

Carter, Jimmy 27

CBO 46,47,48,59,65

CCC 15

Centralized Government Authority 15

Cheney, Dick 59

Climate Change 21,22,67,68

Clinton, Bill 30,35,38,39

COLA 46

CO2 Levels of Ocean 21

Commander-in-Chief 68

Commerce Clause 12

Communism 26

Conservative Agenda 1,67,69,70

Conservative Control 49

Conservative Facts 71

Conservative Ideology 18,19,25

Conservative Kool-Aid 61

Conservative Opinions 71

Conservative Tactics 22,42

Constitution 11,12

Coolidge, Calvin 3,10,11 12,15,36

Cost of Living 60

Countrywide 6,7

Credit Default Swaps 6,44

Cut Spending 36

Cut Taxes 36

D

Dams 48

Debt 69

Defensive Measures(rising oceans) 21,22

Democrat Presidents 39

Designer Mortgages 23,43,44

Dime Savings Bank 9

Disabled 25

Distribution of Wealth 62

Dodd/Frank 42

Dow Jones 39

E

Economic Downturn 34

Einstein, Albert xi,62

Eisenhower, Dwight 37

Employment 21st century 62

Entitlement Programs 33

Evolution 22

F

Family Planning 54

Fannie-May 24,44

Fast Food Industry 53

FDIC 10,45,50

Federal Reserve 10,31,45,50

Federal Employees 45,46

Federalism 12

Federal Regulation 36

Filibuster 33,34,66

Fiscal Conservative 30

Fortune 500 Corporations 45

Food Stamps 46,51,54

Founding Fathers 54

Fox in the hen house 42

Fraud 64

Franken, Al 33,34

Freddie-Mac 24,44

Free Market 18,25,36

Free Will 20

Funding Social Security 63,69

G

Gas tax 66,67

Gates, Bill 32

Gay Rights 25,54

GDP 28,39,40,41,48,65

Global Warming 21,22,67,68

God-given choice 55

Golden Age 36

Goldman Sacks 7

Gould, Jay 1

Government Workers 45

Gramm, Phil 6

Great Depression 7, 10-12, 15-18, 23, 24, 37, 38, 45, 50, 69, 70, 71

Greed 36,37

Greenspan, Allen 31,32

H

Harvard University 31

Heterosexual 20

Highway Trust Fund 66

Hoover, Herbert 3,10-15,17,36

Home Depot 49

Homeownership 42,43

Hooverville's 15,16

House Budgets 35,36

Hunt Brothers 6

Hubris of the U.S. 59

Hussein, Saddam 58

I

Immigration Reform 65

Infrastructure Repair 34,47,48,66,68

Inflation 53

Insurance Restrictions 56

Interstate Highway System 37

Iran 60

Iraq War 32,57,58,59,60,61

Islamic Factions 58

J

Job Growth 35,38,39

K

Kennedy, Ted 34
Koch Brothers 49

L

Laissez-faire 15
Lame Duck 35
Langdon, Kenneth 49
Least Government 42
Lehigh University 5
Less Regulation 36,41
Libertarians 26
Life, Liberty and the Pursuit
    of Happiness 54, 62
Lower Taxes 41
Low Income Americans 54

M

Marginal Propensity to Consume 53
Market Crash 8
Meteorologist 68
Medicaid 51
Medicare 56,63,69

Middle East 57,58,60
Middle Income Americans 70
Military Power 57
Military Threat from Iraq in 2003 58
Military Spending 38
Minimum Wage 53,54,63,69
Minnesota Senate Seat (Al Franken) 33,
    34
Moody 43
Morgan, Pierpont 1
Mortgage Brokers 42
Mortgage Bundles 43,44
Mortgage Crisis 41,42
Mortgage Originators 42
Multibillionaires 49

N

National Debt 28,29,31-33,35,67,70,71
Near Depression 36,49
New Policy to fix problems 68,69
Neocons 19,57,60
No-Doc Loans 23,24,43
Nun on the Bus 52

O

Obama, Barack 33-35,40,49,66
Obamacare 56
OECD 65

Office of Personnel Management 45

OMB 28

Opinions, Conservative 71

Oversight 42

P

Packer, Asa 5

Paulson, Secretary 17

Pay as we go 47

Philanthropy 5

Pillars of Economic Conservatism 25

Planned Parenthood   20,51

Pledge of Allegiance 11

Polar Caps 68

Ponzi Schemes 6,44

Poor 25

Power Transmission 48

Pre 2000 Taxes 47

Pre-existing Conditions 56

Presidential campaign – 1980 25

Presidential Race 2016 55

Private Sector Jobs 35

Privatize Social Security 63

Projected Surplus 31

PTSD 59

R

Rabell-Gonzalez xiv

Read my Lips GHWB 30

Reagan, Ronald 26-31,33,67,70

Reaganomics 26,28,29,31

Reagan Tax Cuts 30

Rebuilding Infrastructure 66

Regulation 36

Religious Zealots 67

Relive Great Depression of 1933 71

Relive Near depression of 2009   71

Republican Governors 51

Republican House 36

Republican Presidents 39

Right to Choose 55

Robber Barons 1,3,5,11

Rockefeller Foundation 5

Rockefeller, John D 1,2,5

Role of Government 19

Roman Catholic 52

Romney, Mitt 47,65

Roosevelt, Franklin D   11

Roosevelt, Teddy 1,3,4

Rubio, Marco 68

Ryan Budget 36,52

S

Safety Net 49

Sands Corporation   49

Satellite images 68

Saying No 63

SEC 44

Second World War 15,27,37

Securities Markets 36

Securities Regulations 37

Senate Banking Committee 6

Senate Rules 70

Sewer Systems 48

Shanty Towns 8

Silver Manipulation 6

Size of Government 25,45

SNAP (Food Stamps) xiii

Social Issues 51,56

Social Security 28,33,63

Social Upheaval 71

Soviet Union 30

Space Program 38

Special Election 34

Speculation (Securities) 36

Standard & Poor 43

Stimulus Package 34,35

Stock Market 10,38

Supply-Side Economics 25,26,32,33,35

Syria 60

Tax Burden 35,65

Tax Freedom Day 65

Tax Cheats 65

Tax Cut -1981 29

Tax Cuts – 2001 & 2003 32,59,64

Tax Increases (Reagan) 29

Tax Increases (Bush 41) 30

Tax Loopholes 3,64

Tax Reform 64

Terrorism 26

Transcontinental Railroad 4,5

Treasury Department 28

Trickle-Down Economics 25,29

Truman, Harry S 39

U

Unbridled Misuse of Power 8

Unbridled Speculation 14

Unemployment Rate 7,51

Unsound Mortgages 24,43

V

VA Costs 59

Vanderbilt, Cornelius 1

T

Taft, William H. 3

TARP 7,17,18,50

W

War Spending 59,60

Water Systems 48

Wealthy Conservatives 49

Woman's Health 25

WPA 15

Printed in the United States
By Bookmasters